Montem Primary School
Hornsey Road
London N7 7QT
Tel: 0171 272 6556
Fax: 0171 272 1838

Watching the Weather

Dew and Frost

Elizabeth Miles

www.heinemann.co.uk/library

To order:
☎ Phone 44 (0) 1865 888066
▤ Send a fax to 44 (0) 1865 314091
▢ Visit the Heinemann Bookshop at www.heinemann.co.uk/library to browse our catalogue and order online.

First published in Great Britain by Heinemann Library, Halley Court, Jordan Hill, Oxford OX2 8EJ, part of Harcourt Education.
Heinemann is a registered trademark of Harcourt Education Ltd.

Editorial: Nicole Irving and Tanvi Rai
Design: Richard Parker and Celia Jones
Illustrations: Jeff Edwards
Picture Research: Rebecca Sodergren and Mica Brancic
Production: Séverine Ribierre

Originated by Dot Gradations Ltd.
Printed and bound in China by South China Printing Company

ISBN 0 431 19023 2
09 08 07 06 05
10 9 8 7 6 5 4 3 2 1

British Library Cataloguing in Publication Data

Miles, Elizabeth
  Dew and Frost. – (Watching the weather)
  551.5'744

A full catalogue record for this book is available from the British Library.

Acknowledgements

The Publishers would like to thank the following for permission to reproduce photographs: Getty Images/Image Bank; Getty Images/PhotoDisc p. i; Alamy Images pp. 4, 5, 15, 17, 20, 21, 27; Comstock p. 11; Corbis/Craig Tuttle p. 7; Corbis/Douglas Peebles p. 16; Corbis/Ecoscene/Andrew Brown p. 19; Corbis/Galen Rowell p. 25; Corbis/Michael Busselle p. 8; Corbis/Lee Cohen p. 23; Getty images/Photodisc pp. 9, 12; Harcourt Education Ltd/Tudor Photography pp. 28, 29; NHPA/Anthony Bannister p. 14; OSF/Olivier Grunewald p. 26; Photofusion/Paul Risdale p. 13; Powerstock/Paco Elvira p. 18; SPL/Astrid & Hans-Frieder Michler p. 24; Travel Ink p. 10.

Cover photographs of dew and frost reproduced with permission of Getty Images/Image Bank; Getty Images/PhotoDisc.

The Publishers would like to thank Daniel Ogden for his assistance in the preparation of this book.

Every effort has been made to contact copyright holders of any material reproduced in this book. Any omissions will be rectified in subsequent printings if notice is given to the Publishers.

The paper used to print this book comes from sustainable resources.

Contents

Any words appearing in the text in bold, **like this**, are explained in the Glossary.

 Find out more about dew and frost at www.heinemannexplore.co.uk

What is dew?

Early in the morning, lawns, trees and cars are sometimes wet. This can happen even when it has not rained. They are wet because of dew.

Tiny drops of water may cover things outside. These drops of water are called dew. Sometimes you can see them shining in the early morning Sun.

Where does dew come from?

Dew comes from water in the air. Water that is part of the air is called **water vapour**. At night, the ground and air get cooler. Then water vapour can turn into dew.

Air above the ground cools

Ground cools at night

Dew drops form

Dew does not fall from the sky like rain. The way in which dew forms is called **condensation**.

Dew can form on cold things, even a spider's web.

We cannot see the water in water vapour. When water vapour turns into dew, it becomes **droplets** of water that we can see.

What is frost?

Sometimes, frost looks a bit like snow.

After a very cold night, the ground may have a white covering of frost. A covering of frost is sometimes called hoarfrost.

Frost is made up of lots of tiny **ice crystals**.
The crystals are **water vapour** that has
frozen. They are so small that you can only
see them clearly through a **microscope**.

In frost, each tiny
ice crystal has a
similar shape.

Where does frost come from?

Frost can form on the ground and trees on cold days.

Like dew, frost comes from **water vapour** in the air. Frost forms when the air touches things that are very cold. The water vapour **freezes** into **ice crystals** on these cold things.

Frost forms when the **temperature** of the ground goes down to below 0°C. (You say below zero degrees centigrade.) At this temperature water vapour freezes into frost.

below 0°C
(32°F)

A thermometer tells us how hot or cold something is. This thermometer shows the temperature at which frost forms.

Frosty patterns and shapes

Frost forms different patterns and shapes. In winter, frost can form patterns on windows. These patterns sometimes look a bit like plant leaves.

This is called fern frost. It looks like the leaves of a fern plant.

Rime is made of frozen water droplets from mist or fog.

Fog and mist can carry very cold **droplets** of water. When wind blows these droplets on to things that are below 0°C, they **freeze** into **ice crystals**. This type of frost is called rime.

Dew, frost and animals

Dewdrops form on the beetle's back. When the drops run down its leg it can drink them.

Animals need water to live. In hot deserts there is very little water, so some animals drink dew. This beetle drinks dew to stay alive.

Animals can drink dew but not frost. In frosty places, birds and other animals may not have any water to drink. They cannot drink the frost until it **melts** into water.

Frost is **frozen** water, so animals cannot drink it.

Dew, frost and plants

Some plants live high up in **rainforest** trees. They cannot get water from **soil** as most plants do. Instead, they take in dew, **water vapour** or falling rain.

Plants need water to live. This plant collects dew in a cup formed by its leaves.

Trees with narrow, needle-shaped leaves are called conifers. Most conifers grow well in places where there is lots of frost.

In frosty winter weather, the leaves on many plants die and drop off. Other plants have special leaves that can live through frosty weather.

Frosty problems

Frosty, cold weather can cause all kinds of problems. In cold weather, we should keep ourselves warm by wearing lots of clothes and by moving around.

Frost can make the ground slippery so we have to walk carefully.

These winter crops are being grown under big plastic sheets. This saves them from frost.

Frost can damage **crops**. Farmers sometimes protect crops from frost by using heaters or fires. These keep the air around the plants and the ground warm.

The big freeze

Driving fast on black ice causes accidents.

In very cold weather, frost or dew on roads may become a sheet of ice. This ice makes the road very slippery. It is called black ice because the black road shows through it.

Black ice is very dangerous because drivers cannot see it. On television and radio, **weather forecasters** warn people of black ice.

Special trucks throw **grit** on to roads to stop dangerous black ice forming.

Is it frost?

Freezing water can break rocks. This is called frost wedging. Although it has frost in its name, frost wedging is not caused by frost. It happens when water freezes in cracks.

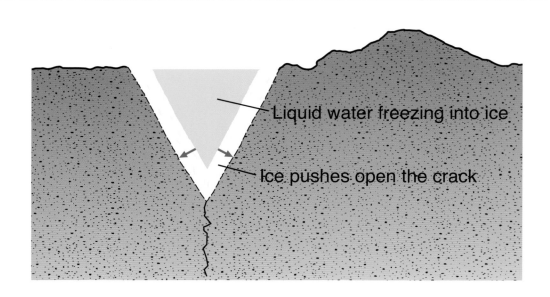

Liquid water freezing into ice

Ice pushes open the crack

As water freezes, it takes up more space and makes the crack bigger.

Frost wedging can make rocks fall. Mountain climbers wear a helmet to help keep them safe.

Frost wedging happens a lot on mountains. It can break big rocks apart. The broken rocks often fall down the mountainside.

Not really frost

These tomatoes have been damaged by black frost.

Black frost is not really frost. It is not made of **water vapour** that has **frozen**. Black frost is when the water inside living plants **freezes**.

Frostbite is not caused by frost. It is when part of someone's body freezes. People can lose their toes because of frostbite.

Mountain tops are very cold places. Mountain climbers must be warmly dressed so that they do not get frostbite.

Permafrost

Even though permafrost has the word frost in its name, it is not frost at all. Permafrost is **frozen** ground that stays frozen all year.

Trees do not grow in permafrost. Only grasses and other small plants can grow.

These people live in a very cold part of Canada where there is permafrost.

It gets very cold in places where there is permafrost. People must be very warmly dressed when they go outside.

Project: water from the air

This project shows you how to make your own drops of water from **water vapour**.

You will need:
- a drinks can
- fridge
- warm room

1. Put a drinks can in a fridge and leave it there for about 3 hours.

2. Take the cold drinks can out of the fridge and put it in a warm room.

3. Watch what happens. Drops of water should form on the can.

4. Why do you think this happens?

> ### What happens?
> A warm room has lots of water vapour in the air. The water vapour changes into drops of water when it touches the cold can. This is called **condensation**.

Find out more about dew and frost at www.heinemannexplore.co.uk

Glossary

condensation way water vapour turns into drops of water, or dew

crops plants that farmers grow, such as cereals, vegetables and fruit

droplets very small drops of a liquid such as water

freeze turn into a very cold solid. For example, water freezes into ice.

frozen when water vapour or liquid water has turned into solid ice

grit tiny bits of stone

ice crystals tiny bits of water that are frozen solid

melts when heat turns a solid into a liquid, like ice into water

microscope instrument to make tiny things look bigger so we can see them better

rainforest jungle where lots of rain falls

soil also called earth or mud. Soil is made up of lots of different things, including tiny bits of rock and dead plants.

temperature how hot or cold something is

water vapour tiny droplets of water that are part of the air around us. The droplets are so tiny and light that they can float in the air.

weather forecasters people who study the weather and work out what the weather might be like

Find out more

More books to read

My World of Science: Water, Angela Royston
(Heinemann Library, 2001)

Geography Starts Here! Weather Around You, Angela
Royston (Hodder Wayland, 2001)

What is Weather? Watching the Weather, Miranda
Ashwell and Andy Owen (Heinemann Library, 1999)

Websites to visit

http://www.weatherwizkids.com
A website packed with information about weather
features, satellite images from space, games and fun
activities to do with the weather.

http://www.planetpals.com/weather.html
Learn more about different sorts of weather and
interesting weather facts to share with friends.

Index

Titles in the *Watching the Weather* series include:

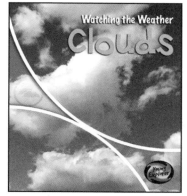

Hardback   0 431 19022 4

Hardback   0 431 19023 2

Hardback   0 431 19024 0

Hardback   0 431 19025 9

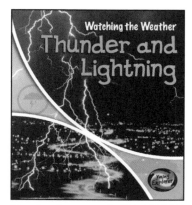

Hardback   0 431 19026 7

Find out about the other titles in this series on our website www.heinemann.co.uk/library